GW00371945

This edition copyright © 2003 Lion Publishing
Text copyright © 1997 Tom Wright

The author asserts the moral right to be identified
as the author of this work

Published by
Lion Publishing plc
Mayfield House, 256 Banbury Road,
Oxford OX2 7DH, England
www.lion-publishing.co.uk
ISBN 0 7459 4673 9

First edition 1997 (published as
A Moment of Prayer, A Moment of Peace, A Moment of Quiet)
10 9 8 7 6 5 4 3 2 1

All rights reserved

A catalogue record for this book is available
from the British Library

Typeset in Goudy OldStyle
Printed and bound in Singapore

quiet moments

Tom Wright

LION
Giftlines

Silence is...

S i l e n c e *is...*

the deep well

from which

we can draw

living water.

Silence is...
 the gentle kiss
that tells us
 it's all right
to relax now.

Silence is...
the long sigh
at the end of
the symphony.

Silence is…

the total rest when

all passion is spent

Silence is…
the sense of calm
when all the tears
have been cried.

Silence is…
the gift of
a gentle mother
to her weary
children.

Silence is…
the clean canvas
on which
the divine artist
paints a fresh vision
of his own image.

Silence

is...

the only way

to hear the music

of the angels.

I love
quietness

I love quietness…
because there
comes a time
when the chattering
of my voice
stops me hearing
what I'm saying.

I love quietness…
because there
comes a time
when the babble
of my voice
stops me hearing
what I'm thinking.

I love quietness…
because there
comes a time
when the prattling
of my voice
stops me hearing
what God is saying.

*I love quietness…
because there comes a
time when the happy
noise of human speech
stops me hearing the
soft crying of humans
in pain.*

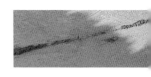

*I love quietness…
because there comes a
time when the warm
blanket of speech is so
cosy that my mind goes
to sleep.*

I love quietness...
because there comes a
time when I realize I don't
know what to say any
more, and when I realize
that it doesn't matter.

I love quietness…
because when God gave us
one mouth and two ears,

he probably intended us
to use them in that proportion.

I love quietness…
because it brings me
through the whirlwind
to the stillness
which is at its centre.

stillness in busy lives

The command:
'Stop, look, listen!'
is good advice for
someone about to
cross a road.

It's even better advice
for someone who wants
to cross the threshold
into the presence of God.

Darkness gives
the eyes
rest from
the glaring
of light

Stillness gives
the ears and mind
rest from
the glaring
of noise

It is part of being truly human that we should create for ourselves oases of stillness in which we can be refreshed.

If I don't
keep still
and shut up,
I won't hear
the music.

The perfect
love of God
casts out fear,
including the
fear of stillness
that drives people
to the Walkman,
the ghettoblaster
and the muzak.

When you see
the Matterhorn
for the first time,
all words seem feeble.
What about when
you sense the love
of God?

If we always
have to say things
out loud,
there's no room
for mystery
or imagination.

Sometimes
  I'm too tired
to think of the words,
  too busy
to get them straight,
  or too anxious
to think of
  something appropriate.

The workaholic
needs to stop
  sometimes;
so does his
spiritual equivalent.

Quiet **moments**

Savour the moment...
when the restless
child has finally
gone to
sleep.

Savour the moment…
when the rain stops,
the wind drops,
and the countryside
is suddenly still.

Savour the moment…
when the storm subsides
and the sea is calm.

Savour the moment...
when the last echo
dies away
and the music
becomes a memory.

Savour the moment...
when the car stops,
the engine is turned off,
and we have arrived
at last.

The
silence
of
eternity

Beyond

words...

there is a country

with a different sort

of language

altogether.

Beyond words…
there is a welcome
in which open arms
and eyes full of love
say everything that
needs to be said.

Beyond words…
there is a forgiveness
that is offered
with no need for
explanations or excuses.

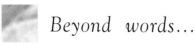 *Beyond words...*
there is a truth that
cannot be stated,
debated, proved, or
explained, but only
known and loved.

Beyond words…
there is a world
to which books
can point, but
which books can
never describe.

Beyond words…
there are actions
which speak
more deeply and truly
than anything
we could say.

In *returning*
and rest
you shall be saved;
in quietness
and confidence
shall be
your strength.

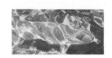

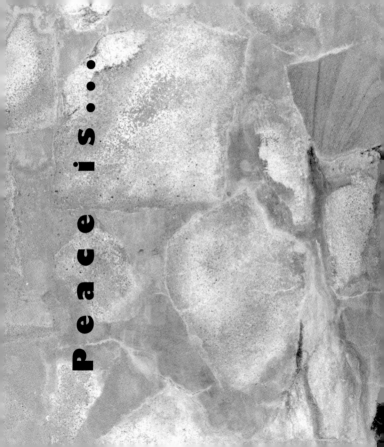
Peace is...

Peace is…

built on the rock

of God's
love.

Peace is...

not a matter of

thinking how bad I am,

but of realizing

how much God loves me.

Peace is...

not sorting myself out,

but letting God

sort me out.

Peace is…

not bullying myself

into submission,

but allowing God

to tell me the truth.

Peace is…
glimpsing
the beauty of God,
and stopping
to gaze in wonder.

Peace is…
sensing
the love of God,
and opening up
to it like a flower
in the sunshine.

Peace is…
the sigh of relief
when I stop
hiding
from God
at last.

Peace with God…
when God looks
straight into my eyes
and says:
'Since I love you,
why don't we
talk about it?'

Peace with God…
is all of me
in the presence
of God.

.   *Peace with God…*
is all of God
into the depths
of me.

confession

Confession…

is an act of

realism,

recognizing

myself as

I really am.

Confession...
is an act of humility,
abandoning pride.

Confession...
is an act of faith,
knowing that if
I cast myself
on God's mercy
he won't let me drop.

Confession…

is climbing down
off the pedestal of
my own self-importance,
and standing on
the level ground
of God's evaluation
of me.

Confession...

*depends on
believing that God
is an infinitely loving
and merciful God,
who likes nothing better
than to forgive.*

Confession...

*because when you
walk along the street
your feet get dusty,
and it's good
to wash them
when you come
into the house.*

Confession...

*because you can't
maintain a friendship
if there's a
mounting backlog
of untold secrets.*

A quiet conscience

A quiet conscience…
because if rivers
of living water are
to flow out of my heart,
they must first
flow through it
to rinse it clean.

A quiet conscience…

because regular tidying up

means that spring cleaning

once a year

isn't such hard work.

A quiet conscience…
because if I admit now
that I'm on the wrong road,
it won't be as hard
to get back to the right one
as it will if I go
blundering on for
another few miles.

A quiet conscience…
because excuses merely
make the water
that much muddier.

A quiet conscience…
because hypocrisy
is such hard work
that it's refreshing
to stop pretending
I'm perfect.

A quiet conscience…
because 'sorry' is one of
the most liberating words,
both for the one
who says it
and for the one
to whom it is said.

A quiet conscience…
because taking responsibility
for my thoughts, words and actions
is part of being fully human.

A quiet conscience…
because trying
to hide from God
is itself an act of pride.
It is also a complete
waste of time.

Peace with the world…
because sorting things out
with God
is the best possible prelude
to sorting things out
with each other.

Peace with the world…
because if we got used to
admitting we were
in the wrong as individuals,
the habit might catch on
on a larger scale,
and the results
could be incalculable.

Moments

of

peace

Peace comes when…
I realize
I don't have to
answer back.

Peace comes when...
I slowly inhale
the warm, loving breath
of God.

Peace comes when...
I unclench the fingers
that cling to my own
vision of the future.

Peace comes when…
I take the carefully nursed
resentments out of the
secret, locked drawer
and throw them away.

Peace comes when…
I take the carefully hidden
admirations out of the
other locked drawer
and express them freely.

Peace comes when…
I celebrate
someone else's success
as if it were my own.

Peace comes when…
I celebrate
my own success
as if it were someone else's.

Jesus said:
'Peace is what
I leave with you;
it is my own peace
that I give you.
I do not give it
as the world does.'

Prayer is . . .

Prayer is…
faith asking.

Prayer is…
hope waiting.

Prayer is…
love embracing.

Prayer is…
me being me
in the presence of
God being God.

Prayer is…
God being God
in me
being me.

Prayer is…
the catalyst that means
the experiment will work
at last.

Prayer is…
a glass of wine
poured into a
bowl of water,
suffusing it with
its gentle colour.

Prayer is…
the most
human thing
we can do –
and the most
divine.

Prayer

Prayer…
opens the
locked gate
into the
rose garden.

nor superior.

Prayer…
helps us to
grow to our
proper height,

neither inferior

Prayer…
cleans the mirror
in which
I look at myself,
so that I can
see myself
as others see me,
or even
(God help me)
as God sees me.

Prayer…

removes the

spectacles of

pride and fear

through which

I normally look

at everyone else,

and helps me

see them as

God sees them.

Prayer…

opens up the old wound

which hasn't healed right,

eases in the ointment,

and helps it to heal at last.

Prayer…

takes the tangled ball of wool

and gently untangles it,

without snapping it or cutting it.

I pray

because...

I pray because…
God always intended
to bring humans in
on the act.

I pray because…
I often need
to tell someone things,
and there's no one else
I can tell them to.

I pray because…
I often need
to be told things
that no one else
will tell me.

I pray because…
the natural focus
of the sight of
a newborn child
is the distance between
the mother's breast
and the mother's eyes.

I pray because…
the natural longing
of the growing child
is to spend time
with her father.

Praying
in
words

Praying in words…
because words
not only articulate praise –
they become praise.

Praying in words…
because words
not only describe beauty –
they become beauty.

Praying in words…
because words
not only clothe prayer –
they become prayer.

Praying in words…
because until I've said it
I don't always know
what I was thinking
or feeling.

Praying in words…
because God treats us
as children, not
as pet animals.

Praying in words…
because without words
we can fool ourselves
with half-truths.

Praying in words…
because without words
ritual can
become magic.

Praying in words…
because without words
silence can
become meaningless.

A
moment
of **prayer**

A moment of prayer…
when the pain
is sharper even
than I'd feared.

A moment of prayer…

when sudden joy

washes over me

like a tidal wave.

A moment of prayer…
when I realize
I've stepped off
the cliff of my
own resources, and
without God's help
I'm lost.

We come together

We come together…
as an act of love,
since my sisters and brothers
need me as much as
I need them.

We come together…
as an act of humility,
abandoning our

                        isolation

and self-sufficiency.

We come together…
because if my candle
is to stay alight,
it helps if it's
in a line of
other candles,
and in a place
where the fire
has descended before.